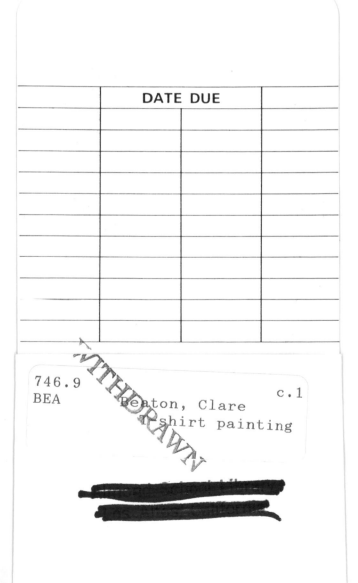

T-SHIRT PAINTING

Devised and illustrated by

Clare Beaton

c.l

WARWICK PRESS

Contents

Produced by
Tony Potter, Times Four Publishing Ltd

Published by Warwick Press, 387 Park Avenue South,
New York, New York 10016, in 1990
Paperback edition published by Franklin Watts,
387 Park Avenue S., NY, NY.

First published in 1990 by Grisewood & Dempsey Ltd,
London.

Typeset by TDR Photoset, Dartford
Colour separations by RCS Graphics Ltd
Printed in Spain

Conception and editorial:
Catherine Bruzzone, Multi Lingua

Library of Congress Cataloging-in-Publication Data

Beaton, Clare.
  T-shirt painting / Clare Beaton.
    p. cm. – (Make and play)
    Summary: Examines various designs for T-shirts and the mat
  and techniques necessary for creating them.
    ISBN 0–531–15164–6   ISBN 0–531–19099–4 (lib. bdg.)
    1. Textile painting – Juvenile literature. 2. T-shirts – Juvenile
  literature. [1. T-shirts. 2. Textile crafts. 3. Handicraft.]
  I. Title. II. Title: Tee shirt painting. III. Series: Beaton,
  Clare. Make and play.
  TT851.B43 1990
  746.9'2–dc20

90–1

About this book

This book will show you some easy and fun ways to decorate your T-shirts. There are step-by-step instructions for painting seven main T-shirts and, at the end of the book, extra ideas for decorating other things made of material.

On the left-hand pages, there are four simple steps to follow:

On the right-hand pages, there is the finished T-shirt with some extra suggestions for you to try:

The simplest designs are at the beginning of the book and the more complicated ones at the end. Fabric paints can be found in most good toy stores, some gift stores, and in stores selling artists' materials.

Look at pages 4-7 for some more helpful hints. The ideas at the end of the book do not have step-by-step instructions but the designs can be painted in similar ways to the main ones. Look back through the book if you need help.

Warning

With this book, older children should be able to paint all but the most complicated designs on their own. However, they may need adult help occasionally and younger children may need help and supervision. Look for special non-toxic fabric paint and take special care with tools like irons, scissors, staplers, and knives. It is worthwhile teaching children to use tools such as craft knives correctly and safely right from the start. Craft knives with blades which retract into the handle are recommended, as are round-ended scissors.

Take extra care where you see this symbol:

Materials

There are lots of different kinds of pens, crayons, paints, and pastels you can buy to decorate clothes and materials. Throughout this book a pen is shown in the instructions, but all the designs, except for printing, could use any of the types of paint shown below. See which you like best and which work best for you.

Colors

When you choose your colors, try to think of the pictures you may draw and which colors will be most useful. Black and bright colors look good on white and pale colored clothes but you may need white on black or darker colors. If you have only two or three colors, make sure they look nice together.

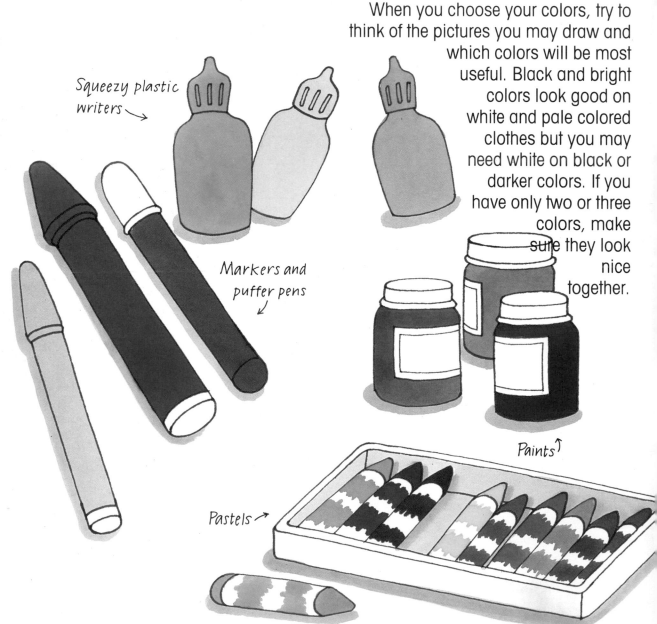

Squeezy plastic writers →

Markers and puffer pens ↓

Paints ↑

Pastels →

4

Materials

Cotton materials with smooth surfaces are best for painting. Some fabric paints will not work at all on nylon, rayon, and so on. Check the label before you buy the paint.

Clothes to use

Look for old or cheap T-shirts at rummage sales or charity shops. If they are secondhand, give them a good wash before you use them. Some cheap T-shirts may have buttons, but you can use them in your design. Don't forget undershirts, both with and without sleeves can be used.

Banner

Picture

Flag

Old sheets or pillowcases can be cut up and made into a variety of things.

Cushion

Hints and tips

All the different paints you can use to decorate your T-shirt will have different instructions for use. Read the labels carefully before you buy them to make sure they are suitable for whatever you want to paint. Sometimes you need to wash and dry the material before you begin. If so, do that well in advance. It's a good idea to wash and dry some old white hankies or pieces of sheet. You can use these to try out your paints before decorating T-shirts and other clothes.

Ironing

You may need an iron to fix your drawing. This will stop it from running or fading when the material is washed. Ask an adult to do this for you.

Check on the instructions whether or not you need to put a piece of plain material or paper over the painting before ironing.

Drawing

Before you start your drawing, think how you want it to look and, if possible, draw it out first on paper. Make your rough drawing very simple as you will find that simple drawings are easier to paint on the material. If you make a mistake on the T-shirt, you can't rub it out!

Don't forget!

Most T-shirt paints soak through to the back of the material. Here is how to avoid ruining the back of your T-shirt.

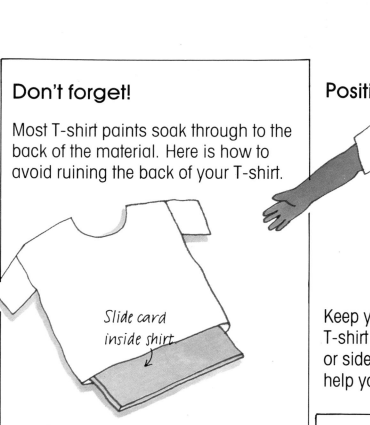

Slide card inside shirt

Push a piece of cardboard or thick paper inside the T-shirt before you start, to give a flat surface and to prevent any paint going through to the back. Leave it in until the painting is dry.

What looks best

The designs will look best if they are large, colorful and bold rather than small and detailed. Don't expect your pictures to be perfect copies of the ones in this book. See if you can think of some ideas of your own too.

Position

Keep your drawing in the center of your T-shirt and not too near the neck, bottom or sides. Look at your rough drawing to help you decide where to start painting.

Front and back

Front

Back

If you want to paint a design on the back or sleeves as well, wait until the front is completely dry. Don't forget to slide a clean piece of cardboard inside the shirt.

Lion

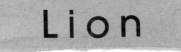

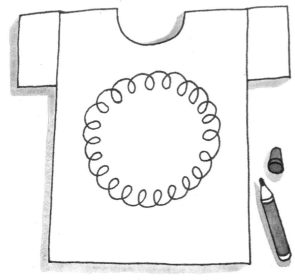

1 Draw the outline of a lion's mane in black. Use a plate to get a neat circle.

2 When dry, use yellow paint to color in the outline.

3 Leave it to dry again. Now draw the lion's head in the middle.

4 Last of all paint the lion's tongue in red.

You can decorate the edge of the sleeves and neck with a different color

Tom

Sign your name if you like.

Face

1 Whether you draw your own face or someone else's, first have a good long look at it.

2 Then draw a face outline.

3 Draw in the eyes, nose, mouth, and hair.

4 Finish by drawing in any special details such as glasses, freckles, beard or earrings.

Give your best friend a
present of a T-shirt with
their face drawn on it.

Lucy

Ben

MOM

Write whose face
it is.

Draw down
to the chest
if you like.

Tractor

1 First look at a picture of a tractor, or look at a toy tractor.

2 Draw in the wheels in black.

3 Now draw the body of the tractor in green.

4 Finish the details on the wheels and draw in the driver and exhaust pipe.

You can draw lots of other vehicles too.

Draw some tire tracks in black.

Here are some pictures to copy.

Framed

1 First draw a frame in the color you want.

2 Then draw outlines of the picture you want in black.

3 Color in the outlines as neatly as you can.

4 Finish the picture by coloring in blue sky and green grass.

You can add more decoration around
the frame in different colors.

Message

1 Draw around a large dinner plate in red.

2 Next draw an inner circle around a smaller plate, also in red. Color in between the circles.

← Place a piece of paper over the circle to practice.

3 Practice on a piece of paper, then copy the outline of the word.

4 Fill in the background of the message in black.

Seaside

1 Draw the crab first in red or orange. Color it in carefully.

2 Next draw the shells and the starfish in pink and purple.

3 Draw the seaweed in green and color it in.

4 Last of all, color around everything in yellow. Leave the edges uneven.

If you have a yellow top, use that and leave out the yellow pen.

Add a blue wavy line all around the bottom.

Here are some more ideas for seaside pictures.

Patterns

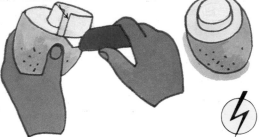

You could use a kitchen knife instead of a craft knife.

1 Cut a medium-sized potato in two. Cut away the potato to make the shape to print.

2 Put some paint in old saucers. Dip the cut potato into it or brush it on.

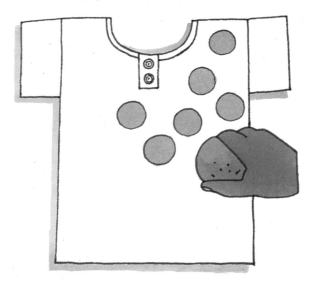

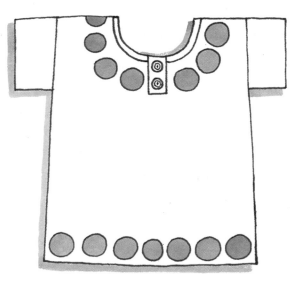

3 Press the potato firmly on to the T-shirt.

4 Try making patterns with your shape.

Try mixing several shapes together in different colors.

Add a leaf and stalk to make a bunch of grapes.

Pillowcases

Draw a picture on a pillowcase.

As well as T-shirts, there are lots of plain cotton things you can draw and paint on, for yourself or to give away as presents.

WELCOME

Banners or flags for a special occasion made from old sheets.

Cut letters or flags out of colored or white cotton. Decorate them and sew them on to tape or string.

← Add colored tape → to make aprons.

Paint small cushions for special occasions. ↓

Paint a meal on an apron.

23

Cut out the material picture and place it on a colored paper background

You could cut the picture with pinking shears.

Draw a picture on a small piece of cotton and mount it in a Clipframe as a present.

Sew the material on to a rod and hang up on a cord.

Sew cut-out pictures on to such things as make-up bags, glasses cases, and tea cosies.

24